But I Don't Know How to ...
Start a Church Library and Archives

by Betty Steele Everett

© 1999 Warner Press, Inc.

Published by Warner Press, P.O. Box 2499, Anderson, IN 46018

All rights reserved.

No part of this book may be reproduced in any form without the written permission of the publisher, except for brief passages included in a review.

All scriptures marked NIV are taken from the HOLY BIBLE: NEW INTERNATIONAL VERSION®. NIV®. Copyright © 1973, 1978, 1984 by International Bible Society. Used by permission of Zondervan Publishing House.

Printed in USA

ISBN 0 87162 852 X

CONTENTS

Chapter 1: From Call to Committee 7

Chapter 2: Help! And Where to Find It 12

Chapter 3: Getting What You Need to Start 17

Chapter 4: Bringing Order to Your Material 24

Chapter 5: Set the Rules Early 29

Chapter 6: The "Grand Opening" 33

Chapter 7: Expanding Your Library 38

Chapter 8: Looking to the Future 43

Appendix A: Church Library Associations 46

Appendix B: Deed of Gift Sample Form 47

Introducing
Betty Steele Everett

Betty Steele Everett has been interested in church libraries for many years and has helped to start them in different churches. She has also had opportunity to speak to audiences of church librarians.

As a writer, Ms. Everett has published more than 4,000 short stories, articles and devotions. She has also had eight books published, in addition to this one. They include biographies of Billy Sunday, William Wilberforce, Grace Livingston Hill and Ira Sankey.

Betty and her husband, Horace, live in Defiance, Ohio, and have two children and four grandchildren.

Chapter One

FROM CALL TO COMMITTEE

For some time you've had a nagging feeling that the Lord wants you to start ... and maintain ... a library in your church. You love to read, but a library, especially one that includes archives of the church's history, looks like too big a job.

You pray about it, then give yourself ... and God ... every argument you can come up with why someone else should do it.

You point out, very meekly, that all you know about libraries is how to hand a book to the librarian at the public library. As for archives, you're not even sure how to spell it, let alone try to set one up. You think your excuses make those Moses gave to keep from going before Pharaoh look minor league.

Yet the feeling has stayed, stronger than ever. You're sure now that the Lord means for *you* to get to work on this project for Him and His people. So, what's next?

Don't Keep Your Idea a Secret ... Call a Meeting
You can't take on a project this big alone; you're going to need help and lots of it. So, after more prayer, look for help.

- Talk to others in your congregation.

- Talk to your pastor, Sunday school superintendent, youth leader and the heads of the various committees in the church.

- Set a time and place for a meeting of everyone interested in the project and ask groups to send representatives.

Be Ready to Explain Your Project ... and to Deflect Objections
At the meeting ...

- Explain how you feel a church library, and archives as well, would be beneficial to those who attend your church.

- Point out that with a library right in the church, it will be easier to get the right material to the right person at the right time.

- Be prepared for opposition; it's always easier to find fault with someone else's idea than to get involved.

Objections You May Hear, and Possible Answers
Question:
"Why do we need a church library? People have the big one downtown. And we have two bookstores in town, one of them Christian. There are racks of paperbacks in every supermarket and drug store. People can buy their own books. We don't need a library in the church!"

Answers:
- Be ready by writing out a statement of your purpose. Point out that a church library is there to win people to Christ, and to educate and help Christians already dedicated to the Lord to grow in their faith and daily living for Him.

- It will also provide recreational reading of a Christian nature; reading good material always improves the mind in general, and Christians who are good stewards want to develop their minds for Christ's purposes.

- Through a church library, the church is taken out of a building and into people's homes all over your town.

- Most of the books in the places mentioned in the questions are not Christian. A few are, of course, but they are in the minority and may not be the book someone needs right now.

- At this first meeting, have a printout of the Christian books at the local library. These, you stress, will not be duplicated in the church library.

- Also, remind the group that most people can't afford to buy a lot of books, but will read ones that are free to them.

Question:
"What in the world are archives? Sounds really boring to me!"

Answer:
- Don't let the academic title "archives" throw you. It's just a big, important sounding name for things from the past that are of interest today. In a church the archives would include anything that tells the story of your church from its beginning: bulletins, record books, photographs and any other papers or items that were important as your church moved ahead.

Question:
"We're a new church. What do we need with archives? We don't have anything to put in it. That's for old churches!"

Or the opposite: *"We're an old church. No one kept anything from 'way back. Besides, all that stuff is probably lost by now. Why should we even try to find it?"*

Answers:
- The answer to the first is that a new church has a wonderful chance to build archives from the start. There will be no "gaps" in its history for people to wonder about fifty years from now.

- Old churches need to have as much of their history saved and available as possible so that today's members can appreciate what's gone on before. (More on this in Chapter 3.)

Question:
"We don't have any room for a library or archives. Every inch of our church is in use now. Where would you put it?"

Answer:
- Since most churches really are cramped for space, this question is sure to come up. Before the meeting, take a long, slow tour of your whole church, not just the sanctuary and Sunday school rooms. Poke into every nook, cranny and alcove. Try to visualize whether it would be adaptable for a library and archives. (More of this in Chapter 3.)

Question:
"We don't have any money for a library or archives. That takes books, shelves and all kinds of stuff."

Answer:
- Unfortunately, money is often the "bottom line" for churches just as it is for other groups and individuals. You will have to be ready with some ideas to suggest to the congregation that will make the cost of starting and maintaining your library and

archives less than they had imagined. (More of this in Chapters 3 and 8.)

Don't Be Turned Off by These Objections

While all of these objections are meant to discourage you, don't let them sap your enthusiasm or certainty of God's leading. At some point, at least one other person will catch the dream and be led by the Lord to offer to help. Embrace him or her! This person or persons is God's gift.

And when one person decides to join you, others will follow. They may not be the people who came to the first meeting, or even the people you expected to come forward, but they will be your "Library and Archives Committee." And, hopefully, they will be as enthused and excited to get started as you are.

Your Committee Should Represent the Whole Church

Ideally, the committee should have members who represent all phases of church membership: women, men, senior citizens, youth and even a child who loves to read. Enthusiasm and eagerness to work are more important than numbers. If the committee gets too large, members feel free to skip meetings or work sessions because "no one will miss me in the crowd."

Time to "Walk the Talk"

You've gotten your call from the Lord and your committee from the church. Now it's time to turn the page and get down to hard work ... and planning.

Chapter Two

HELP! AND WHERE TO FIND IT

You're excited and ready to go. But where are you going? And how do you get there from here? You feel like a car, stalled somewhere in the wilderness with no map to guide you. Moses had a cloud and a pillar of fire, and the Wise Men had a star to show them the way, but you're frustrated. You need help, but where can you find it?

Look in Your Own Congregation

- You may be one of the fortunate churches that has a librarian, either active or retired, in the congregation. If so, make sure she (or he) is on your committee, or is at least willing to be "on call" as a trouble shooting consultant.

- Find out if any of your members, while not a trained librarian, has worked part time there, or volunteers. Listen to these people's advice on setting up the library.

- There may also be a history teacher, college history major, or, more likely, a local history "buff" who can give you advice on developing the archives.

- Among your members are people who have come to your town and church from other places. These other churches may have

had libraries. Listen to their negative thoughts about these libraries, as well as their positive points:
- *"It was way upstairs in a tiny room."*
- *"It wasn't open when I could get there."*
- *"You could only take out one book at a time."*
- *"They didn't have any books I was interested in."*

These remarks can give you clues about what NOT to do, which sometimes is as helpful as knowing what is good to do.

Talk to Other Librarians

Sad to say, the chances are that there won't be a trained librarian in your church. But you are still not alone. There are other librarians in town.

- Talk to the librarians at the public library for tips on setting up your church's library. Write down questions you need answers to and carry this list with you each time.

- Librarians in the schools can suggest reading levels, hints on how to display books to make them more attractive to children and young people, and other things you may not have thought of.

- Other churches' librarians may have been at this awhile. If you don't know which churches in your town already have working libraries, call and ask. You may be surprised to find that the "richest" church has no library or one that has been allowed to die out, while smaller, newer churches may have active libraries.

In all cases, get the names of the people in charge and make an appointment to talk to them ... in their library. When you get there, look the library over carefully. How are the books displayed? How do they handle check-outs and returns? What does the room look like ... is it carpeted, cheerful, well lighted? What furniture do they have? What ideas can you take back to your own church?

Notice, too, if the library has historical (archival) material displayed. If not, ask about archives. Fewer churches have these than have libraries, but many try to keep a running history of their church's work, even if it's just a big scrapbook. Make notes of how archival material is catalogued and displayed.

Don't be discouraged by big, nicely arranged and furnished libraries or archives rooms in other places. They all started just the way you are; they've just had more time to develop their libraries. In a year or so you may be surprised at your own progress.

Other church librarians can tell you what kinds of books and authors are popular with Christian readers. You can expect names like Max Lucado, Marjorie Holmes, and Josh McDowell to come up, but many more very good Christian writers should be considered in stocking your church's library. Other church librarians may make suggestions that will probably include some writers you've never heard of!

In addition to information and tips on what books would be best to have, church librarians can give you ideas on where to buy them. They can also give advice on other materials you might want to consider carrying in your library.

Some big church libraries, like that of Clear Lake United Methodist Church in Houston, Texas, carry a lot more than books. They offer CDs, tapes, videos, film strips and other media materials. All of these are available to members, but additions like this may have to be something for you to dream about and plan for the future; add them to your "wish list."

Your Best Friend ... the Christian Bookstore

If anyone in town knows what books Christians are looking for, it's the owner or manager of your local Christian bookstore. Some of these stores are owned by denominations, a few by corporations, but most are locally owned and operated. They may belong, however, to a group of stores that lets them buy books from publishers in bigger quantities and at bigger discounts.

These people not only know their own stock, but the many other books they don't have the space to carry. They also know the town and what people in your area want to read. Make an appointment to meet with them.

Ask questions like:
- *"What books are most popular?"*
- *"What would you suggest for a 'basic' starting library?"*
- *"How soon can you get books you don't have in stock?"*
- *"What other library supplies do you carry?"*

Don't hesitate to ask about a discount. Most Christian bookstores will give churches from 10 to 25 percent off retail. If you allow them to hold a book fair in your church (more on this in Chapter 8), you may be able to bargain for an even larger percentage of the sales. If in doubt about the benefits your church may receive, ask! You may be surprised at the help that may be offered to you.

Christian bookstores also have the catalogs of all the major (and most minor) Christian publishers. Even a quick study of them will show you what's available out there. The manager of the store can also notify you when a publisher is having a clearance of his "remainder" books. (Remainders are books that remain when the title is taken out of print and no more will be published. They are usually sold at a fraction of the original price.)

Check Historical Societies for Help with Archives

While historical societies usually have a whole house, or at least an entire floor, to display materials, you can get some idea of how they do it. You may even find something relating to your own church's history here, material you might be able to at least photocopy. With today's machines, copies of photos are almost as good as the original.

After all these visits, asking questions and hearing what other people are doing you should feel a lot more confident of being able to handle this call from the Lord. Now you can get to work!

Chapter Three

GETTING WHAT YOU NEED TO START

Now that you know the answers to a lot of your questions, it's time to actually get something concrete going. But it makes no sense to begin stocking books and archival material when you still don't have any place to put them. Where can you put your new library/archives?

What's That in Your Hand?
When God asked Moses this question (Exodus 4:2), He already knew Moses was holding a rod. God wanted to show Moses that what he already had right there was going to be used for a much greater purpose.

In your "hand" is your church building and congregation. Unless you are a new church, or have just put on an addition, a big, comfortable room is probably not sitting empty, just waiting for you to claim it and fill it with books and historical material. You're going to have to find that room!

Remember that tour of the building you took before you met with your committee? Now you and that committee are going to take

But I Don't Know How to ...
Start a Church Library and Archives

another tour. This time you are definitely looking for a place to put your library/archives.

Location, Location, Location

Real estate salespeople know the three most important things in getting a house to sell quickly are "location, location, location." The same is true with a church library. Jesus said, "No one lights a lamp and puts it in a place where it will be hidden, or under a bowl. Instead he puts it on its stand, so that those who come in may see the light" (Luke 11:33 NIV).

You want your library/archives to be a "light" for the congregation to learn more about the Lord and themselves. You have to put it where it can be seen.

No one, for example, and especially older people, want to climb two flights of stairs to visit the library. Out of sight is really out of mind here.

Ideally, your library should be near the sanctuary and Sunday school classrooms, where people pass often. Since there is no empty room waiting for you, you will have to find ways to make one space do the work of two.

Think Creatively

Brainstorm with your committee. Urge everyone to shoot off ideas from the tops of their heads, just as fast as they can think of them. Don't laugh at any ... some ideas may sound weird or quirky at first, but with some adaptations, might work.

Keep your members on track, though, or things can get out of hand (like the suggestion of using a spaceship that would land every Sunday on the church lawn!).

Options to Consider:
- Do you really need a whole room at first? Could you curtain off part of a large room that isn't being used to capacity?

- Can items now stored in different places be combined in one spot? Things like Christmas decorations, office supplies and next quarter's Sunday school papers and books? Right now each of these may be kept in a different place. Can you put them all together? There may be space for them in a Sunday school room, or a part of the fellowship hall.

- Is there a large Sunday school room that could double as a library/archives? This is not the best solution, but it works in some churches. Would some organization be willing to move from a large room to a smaller one, leaving that room for you?

Once you've found your space, start collecting the things to put in it.

Hunt, Find and Divide

Again, use what's in your "hand" to start. Check all the closets, Sunday school storage cabinets, and boxes stacked here and there. Things no longer being used are often just shoved into boxes and put in a tiny basement room or an attic area.

- For the library, you are looking for: Bibles, including children's Bibles; Bible handbooks and commentaries; old Sunday school workbooks and texts; old Vacation Bible School workbooks and texts; hymnals; and any other books that might have been left in the church and forgotten.

- For the archives, look for historical material: old bulletins, correspondence, record books, and photos of church members and activities.

But I Don't Know How to …
Start a Church Library and Archives

Move everything you find into the area where the library/archives will be. Divide your committee with one-half working on the library material, the other half on the archives.

Organize

Divide the books into piles according to their type or subject matter. Do the same with the archival things.

"Don't mix archival materials," says Colleen Warner, archivist from Defiance, Ohio, who has organized archives for several groups in the past. "That is, don't put sermons, bulletins and photos together just because they are all from the same year. Keep bulletins with bulletins, etc."

Not Everything Is Good

God found everything He made was good, but everything you find won't be. Much of what was packed away years ago was packed away because no one was using it, but didn't know what else to do with it. It may still be worthless. Take time to separate the wheat from the chaff.

Diana Coy is the founder of the library and librarian at Calvary Bible Church in Paulding, Ohio. The church library is only a few years old, and Diana has made up a printed statement to let people know what materials can't be used in the library. Anything yellowed, ripped or chewed, musty smelling, water damaged, scribbled or marked or outdated won't be accepted.

"If you would not want to touch it," says Diana, "no one else would want to, either."

That's a good rule to follow for the books you find. Pages missing or other damage means you just have to grit your teeth, close your eyes and toss it out. This is extremely difficult for those of us who

_____ Getting What You Need to Start

hate to throw anything away, but it's wise to draw the line somewhere.

Colleen Warner suggests that for archival material you ask yourself: Does it have any enduring value ... such as minutes from long ago meetings? Does it have any informational value ... such as bulletins which tell what was going on in the church? Does it have any functional value ... like correspondence?

Everything Needs a Home
While you now have a room, or at least part of a room, for your things, you don't have any place for each thing ... no shelves, file folders, boxes, furniture. And no money to buy any.

- Call on your congregation again. Will some individuals or groups give money to help you get started? Can you ask the church's governing board for a small amount? Can you ask to have a special offering in Sunday school or church? One church puts an offering plate at both the front and back of the sanctuary when a special offering is received.

- Naturally, a line amount in the church's yearly budget for the library would be the best solution, but that may have to wait until you are well started and have proved the value of the library/archives. Right now you don't need a large amount of money if you can get other things donated.

- Do any members have bookshelves they aren't using? Can the men's organization build you shelves? If worst comes to worst, make shelves from boards separated by bricks you can paint bright colors. Just ask any college student of a generation ago about these!

- Ask, too, about donations of small tables, a desk, lamps and chairs if you have room for them. These aren't vital to start, but would be nice to have.

Put the shelves against the walls to save space. Borrow a trick from supermarket managers who put highly advertised cereals and other "child friendly" foods on the lower shelves, at a child's eye level. Do the same with books ... put children's books on the lowest shelves where they can easily be seen and reached.

Filling the Shelves

At first the shelves, no matter what kind, will look empty. They are, and you want to fill them as fast as you can, but there are red warning flags.

- "Be careful about asking people to donate books from home," says Millie Hutchinson, librarian at the Defiance, Ohio, First Presbyterian Church, where the library has been working for about 30 years. "People clear off the shelves and give it all to you. A lot isn't what you want."

  Many such donated books are outdated and don't meet the criteria Diana Coy set up. Before you take these, or anything else for the library or archives, have the donor sign a "Deed of Gift." (A sample form is included in Appendix B.)

  A "Deed of Gift" is merely a signed statement that the donor is giving you the materials listed, and that you are free to do with them whatever you feel is best, including dumping them! This protects the church in case there are any questions later.

- Both Millie Hutchinson and Diana Coy agree on the basic books you need in a church library. Bibles (of several versions), concordances, Bible references and handbooks to help members in their study of God's Word should be the foundation of your library. Biographies of Christian men and women and self-help books are also important. Fiction, poetry and other Christian books should be included as quickly as possible.

- Ask those who attend your church to keep an eye out for historical material, too, both in their own homes and outside. One couple who followed flea markets found an old postcard picturing their church. For a dollar they added an interesting bit of history to the archives.

- Keep a "wish list" of books, furniture and other items you'd like to see in the library. Make sure everyone in the church knows about it.

Now it's on to the job of cataloging the items you have gotten so far, so borrowers can quickly find the right book at the right time.

Chapter Four

BRINGING ORDER TO YOUR MATERIAL

You now have enough books to start your library, and some archival material, too. Remembering Paul's advice to the Corinthians, "Let all things be done decently and in order" (1 Corinthians 14:40), you want to find the best way to catalog (index) your material so users can find what they want quickly.

Choose a Simple Cataloging System
If you have a trained librarian on your committee, she (or he) will want to use the popular Dewey Decimal System followed for years in most libraries. Give them the OK. As your library grows, you may be glad you started this way; new additions can be put in the right place immediately.

However, the Dewey Decimal System may be too complicated for your library right now, especially if you don't already have several hundred books. It may also be confusing to volunteers who know nothing about it except that it exists.

The Dewey Decimal System has almost 1000 divisions, each with many sub-divisions. A church library would probably never use all of these, even those in the 200-299 (Religion) series. If you want to use the Dewey method, you can get a copy of it at your public library.

There are more simple, basic systems that you can tailor to your own church, at least at first.

David Everett, Library Director at Hiram College in Ohio, suggests that instead of the Dewey System, each church make up its own list of 10 or 12 categories, depending on the kinds of books they have and hope to have.

"Churches would not all have the same listings," Everett says. "Whatever fits your church is what you want to use."

Some categories you'll have books for are: Bibles, Bible Study Helps (concordances, dictionaries, interpretation), Biography, Children's Books, Denominational, Devotions, Hymnals, Parenting, Self-Help, Adult Fiction and Youth Fiction.

Look over the books you have now, and divide them into categories to help you make up your own listing. When you know what divisions your books fall into, you are ready to prepare them individually for borrowing.

Preparing the Books for Circulation
- Again, keep it simple! Most libraries follow the pattern the public libraries used in the days before the computer took over. Each book has a card in a pocket in back. The card gives the title of the book, its author, and, if you want, a number to show its category. You can also use different colored cards to indicate the book's category.

  Under the lines for the book's title and author, a space is

provided for the borrower's name and the date the book is due back at the library. To find where to buy these supplies, check with your Christian bookstore, your denominational headquarters, or the public library.

- One church uses a small piece of colored tape at the bottom of the spine of each book to show its classification. A red tape means one category, green another. Blue, purple, yellow, orange, brown and black show other types. This makes re-shelving the books easier and allows users to identify divisions more quickly.

  In that library, books in each color group are arranged alphabetically by author on the shelves. A large poster on the wall shows the tape color for each kind of book.

- The library at Calvary Bible Church in Paulding, Ohio, uses the simplest system of all. On a tablet, kept on a shelf inside the door, the borrower writes his name, the title of the book he is taking out, and the date. This works well in a small church and saves the cost of cards and pockets.

- You also need a way to identify the book as belonging to your church library. Then the book will not be mistaken for a public or school library book.

  An inexpensive rubber stamp with your church's name and address solves the problem. Check with your church secretary; the church may already have this stamp.

  Stamp the book on the title page, under the publisher's name, on the bottom of the book pocket (or on the inside of the back cover if you're not using pockets) and on the edges of the book's pages when it is closed.

The Library's Master List

You also need some kind of "master list" for both your books and the material in the archives. Following are a few methods by which to maintain such a list:

- A notebook may be kept with the title, author and date the book or other item was given.

- Better, books can be listed on cards in an old fashioned card catalog form. These can have one or two lines describing the book, which you can easily get from the dust jacket or a quick skimming of the table of contents. Each new book should have a listing here.

- Cards can be kept in a small file box, but both they and the notebook (if you are using that method) must be available to readers who want to know where to find a specific book.

  Separate the cards (or have sections in the notebook) for each category of books, and for the archives material. If you are using color codes for books, put that color along the top edge of the master card.

Is This All There Is?

If your committee has been offered other items for the library (magazines, tapes, Christian CDs, videos, or art), catalog these with the number and perhaps an initial ... e.g. CD-23. Keep a file card or master list of these, as well as putting a pocket (where possible) on the item if that is your system.

Archives Display

- Decide how you want to display your historical material. All paper, including clippings, photos and other items, should be put into acid free folders, with no more than 10 or 12 photos in

But I Don't Know How to ... Start a Church Library and Archives

each folder. The folder can then be labeled "Photos of Church Picnic, 1987," for example.

- "Acid free" is the key to keeping paper material safe for years. The name sounds expensive, but these folders and boxes do not cost much more than ordinary folders and bankers' boxes, depending on the size and how many you buy at a time. Check with your local office supply store, and if they don't carry these, ask the public librarian to let you check the catalogs they have from library and archives supply companies.

- There will be other archival items that are not paper. Some churches celebrated 25th, 50th, or 100th anniversaries with commemorative plates, mugs or spoons. Almost all churches have had cookbooks made up of members' favorite recipes. All these, along with framed portraits of former pastors or other leaders, and models of an old church building, or even Noah's Ark made years ago by a primary Sunday school class can be displayed around the room in various open places. This could be on a wall or the top of bookshelves.

- Beside, or under, the item, write as much information as you have about it, as well as the name of the person who donated it.

- Ask one or two of your committee to be responsible for adding new, current material to the archives. It's good to have historic material, but today's bulletins, meeting minutes, and correspondence will be "historic" in a few years! And it's a lot easier to get this week's bulletin than one from even a month ago. So keep up to date!

Chapter Five

SET THE RULES EARLY

Rules are a part of everyone's life, beginning with God's laws for the early Israelites and Jesus' commandments to His people. While your library rules can't compete with these, your committee will need to come up with rules to keep the library running smoothly. Otherwise, chaos! And no one needs that in a church library.

Who Will Use the Library?
Obviously, the people who attend your church. But what about others in the community? Your church may be the meeting place for groups as varied as Kiwanis, Weight Watchers and Boy Scouts. Will those people be allowed to take books from the church library?

You might want to think twice before you say, "No way!" Letting others besides regular church participants use the library, even at the cost of a few lost books, is an outreach ministry for the Lord.

Many people who come to the church building for other meetings are not church goers, or even Christians. This is especially true of children who may be sent by their parents to Sunday school or Vacation Bible School. If they read some of your books, a big difference could be made in their lives. Every book can be a missionary.

But I Don't Know How to …
Start a Church Library and Archives

If you do decide to let others use your library, be sure to get their names and addresses, along with phone numbers, and impress on them that they are only borrowing the books, not being given them.

When Will the Library Be Open?
A basic decision on this comes down to whether the church library will be open only certain hours, with a volunteer there to help, or unlocked and available whenever the church is open.

Finding a volunteer for more than Sunday morning and maybe an afternoon a week is hard to do, and most church budgets won't stretch to hiring someone.

If the library is to be open whenever the church is, it will have to run on a "self-serve" basis. You can either keep the library door unlocked, or lock it and let the secretary give the key to those who ask for it. This system works for most churches and lets people use the library at their convenience.

In a self-serve library, the reader signs his name, address and date on the card in the back pocket of the book he's taking, then puts the card into a box labeled for them. When he returns the book, he finds the card, scratches out his name, and puts the card back in the pocket. If only a borrower's sheet is used, the reader simply scratches out his name.

Some church librarians ask the returner to re-shelve the book. Others don't want to risk getting a book in the wrong place, so put out another box for returned books, and a volunteer re-shelves several times a month.

How Many Books Can I Take Out?
Decide if you want to set a limit on the number of books that can be borrowed at one time. Some people want more than one,

Set the Rules Early

especially if they are working on a program or talk.

Others think one at a time is plenty. Make a rule, but don't be too strict about enforcing it.

Bring Back My Books!
Set a reasonable length of time for borrowers to keep books. Two weeks for most; maybe only one week for something new and in demand.

What should you do when a book has been kept much too long? The first step is to remind the borrower that he (or she) still has the book they took out a month ago. This can be done in different ways, but every way has to be carefully worded to be sensitive and polite. The reminder should also admit the library could be at fault ... the book wasn't re-shelved right, or someone got the wrong card in it.

Be Tactful
Notices can be given via telephone, postcards or in person. In one church the librarian keeps a running list of late books, and when she sees one of the readers in church, tactfully reminds them. "Tactfully" is the key word! Your library must be user-friendly at all times, even when users aren't library-friendly.

What Do I Owe You?
Sooner or later someone is going to ask what the penalty, or fine, is for an overdue book. Some libraries have found it worthwhile to charge a few cents a day to help get funds for more books.

Most churches, however, do not charge fines. They are just too much work for the money they bring in and the resentment they might cause.

Some churches use an optional system somewhere in between.

There is a small box—a bank in the shape of a church is good—with a label saying it is for fines for overdue books, and that the money will be used to buy more books.

Keep it light, though. Maybe something like: "If your book is overdue, we'd appreciate a dime from you."

When Books Walk Away

Be ready to accept the fact that some books will be taken out and never darken the library shelves again. They are not "stolen," say librarians, just taken out and lost or damaged beyond repair.

Again, "tact" is the key word. No book is worth upsetting someone else over. You may just have to shrug it off and give up on the book if, after a reminder, the book is still AWOL.

Many people will confess they lost the book, or it got destroyed some way, and offer to pay for it. If the book is not a popular one, or one you think is absolutely necessary in the library, you may want to suggest it be replaced with a newer book from your "wish list."

Publish the News

Make sure everyone in the church knows what the library rules are. Post them in the library, and tell volunteers to remind users when they take out books. Periodically, remind members by putting the rules in the church newsletter or bulletin.

Clearly stated rules will keep your library running smoothly.

Chapter Six

THE "GRAND OPENING"

The books are cataloged and neatly arranged on the shelves by type and author. The archival photos and other materials have been sorted, put into acid free file folders, and labeled. The files have been put into acid free storage boxes that are also labeled. In short, you are ready to introduce the library/archives to the whole church: your "Grand Opening."

When Should You Have the Grand Opening?

You want to open the library/archives for the first time with a real attention-getting bang! The Grand Opening should be at a time when most of the people who attend your church will already be in the building, and not have to make a special trip.

- Sunday would seem the logical day. Your committee will have to decide if you want a short opening or a longer one.

- If you think an hour or two is enough, how about the Sunday school hour? Sunday school classes can come to the library one or two at a time to see what's there.

- You might prefer to have the opening right after the worship service, but keep it simple. People are often anxious to get home for dinner or the football game!

What Should Be Part of the Grand Opening?

- No matter what celebration you decide on, begin with a simple dedication service, with prayer and perhaps a hymn as you dedicate the library/archives to the church and the Lord.

- Also take time to introduce the members of your committee and to thank all those involved for the work they have done to prepare the library/archives for the church's use.

- After this, some churches have a coffee hour in the library, but most libraries are not big enough for this. There is the added risk that something will get spilled on the books. However, refreshments are always a big draw for all ages, so you might plan coffee and cookies, served by a women's group in the fellowship hall.

- For a longer opening, you might want to have a "pot luck" ("carry-in banquet," in some places!) for the whole congregation. This gives you more time to show off the library/archives, and gives people a chance to fellowship as long as they want without having to worry about dinner at home. The more people you attract, the better.

- To initiate their library, Diana Coy's church had a "Library Sunday." They invited a Christian writer from the area to talk to the adult and high school Sunday school classes about "Writing as a Ministry."

The writer brought her own books and others she had had a part in, and individuals bought books to donate to the library. It was a good day for both the writer and the new library!

- If you don't know any Christian writers near you, you can ask one of your members to give a review of one of the books instead.

Advertise!

Of course you've been talking up your project all the weeks you've been working on it. Actually, some of your friends may have started to avoid you ... that's a sure sign you're talking too much about it!

All the people who have helped ... building shelves, cataloging books, cleaning the room ... know what is happening. But many in the congregation are only casually aware of what's going on and have not been personally involved.

- Put notices in your church bulletin two or three weeks before the Grand Opening. Put a longer notice in the church newsletter. Try not to make this a dull list of time and place; you want to make people want to come to see what's been going on.

- Write two or three sentences about the aim of the library/archives (something like you had at the first meeting). Or do a short review of the kinds of books and materials you have on hand.

- To advertise the "archives" section and to arouse interest, ask people if they remember a specific event of five, ten or even fifty years ago. Naturally you choose a picnic or meeting you have several photos of, so you can ask people to see who they can identify in them.

    Seeing one's mother (or grandmother!) as a young woman eating watermelon at a church picnic, for example, is bound to bring good memories as well as a laugh at the clothes she's wearing.

But I Don't Know How to …
Start a Church Library and Archives

Having today's members look at photos from years ago means some of the people in the picture will be identified for you.

- Ask young people, or even a children's Sunday school class, to make posters advertising the Grand Opening. Let each "artist" choose their own media and style … humorous, serious, simple, complex. Give everyone the chance to let their creativity flow.

- Ask some of these younger people to make big signs with LIBRARY and an arrow below, pointing the way. If you put these several places in the church, everyone coming in every door will know which direction the library is. These should be left up after the Grand Opening.

Decorate
For your Grand Opening, borrow some ideas from stores and other businesses. Decorate the library. You can use computer-made banners to welcome everyone. Balloons are not expensive and don't have to have helium in them for the time you want them. Pick bright colors and hang them around the room.

In addition, make a display in the library of some of your books. Stand these up on a table, cart or even a window sill as one church does. Choose the books for this carefully. You want something for a variety of ages and interests, and you also want colorful jackets and intriguing titles to grab the visitor's eye.

Hey, Something Free!
Everyone likes to get something for nothing. Have some small item you can give each one who comes to your Grand Opening that will remind them of the library/archives.

A bookmark of bright ribbon or even construction paper, cut with fancy scissors, is easily made by any group in the church, and is inexpensive. If you put a Christian sticker on, and then stamp or type your church's name, it is a library reminder.

Your Christian bookstore probably has other inexpensive ideas, too.

Be Ready to Answer Questions
Even though you've put all the instructions and notices on a wall of the room, and thought you gave all the information in the newsletter and bulletins, people will still have questions. And they prefer having a human to look at as they ask.

Have one of your committee in the library/archives all during the Grand Opening, but the same person doesn't have to be there all the time. They can answer any questions that come up.

There's no argument that a Grand Opening is hard work, but it's also a lot of fun and the perfect way to start your library's ministry.

Chapter Seven

EXPANDING YOUR LIBRARY

Several weeks have passed since your Grand Opening of the library/archives. Many of the books that were eagerly taken out have been returned, and only a few books seem to be moving now. The first enthusiasm seems to be fading.

Don't be surprised at this. Studies show that after an initial burst of zeal for anything new, things go back to what they were. Remember Jesus' parable about the sower? The seeds that fell on stony ground came up quickly, but soon withered.

You want to do something to keep your library from withering.

Is There Any Money?
One of the things you know you need is new books, books that have been published within the last year or two. But it takes money to buy them, even at a discount.

Raising money to keep any church program going is a problem if you haven't been given a place in the overall budget. (More of this in the last chapter.) Of course, if your church has given you a certain amount to spend each year, your problem is how to spend it wisely.

For many churches, though, there is not room in the budget for anything not directly related to the primary ministry of the church. Even if you have been given a line in the church budget, it is often less than you need, so you are on your own to get those new books. Following are some ideas on how to get what you need to keep your library growing.

Memorial Books Can Help Fill the Shelves

One way to get the new books on your "wish list" is to encourage members to give a book to the library in memory of a loved one who has passed away. Put a neatly printed bookplate in the book, telling who it is in memory of and who donated it.

Similar to memorial gifts are "in honor of" gifts for people still living. You can suggest giving a book for a birthday, anniversary or other celebration. A 50th wedding anniversary is a perfect time. By then the couple has all of the material things they need or want, yet people would like to do something to commemorate the big anniversary.

Try to get such books from your "wish list" of basic books because memorial books can never be discarded! They are on the shelves forever.

A notice of any memorial or "in honor of" book donations should be put in the bulletin and newsletter immediately. A note of appreciation should also be sent to the family or individual who is honored, as well as to the donor.

Ask Church Groups for Help

There are many groups in the church: Sunday school classes, women's circles, men's groups, youth groups, choirs, and preschool or school age. Approach them about giving money to buy new books or other things you need.

Suggest books that would go with their age, sex or interests. For example:

- The choir might like a book about hymn writers or the stories behind the hymns they sing.

- The youth group might donate a book on coping as a Christian at school.

- The women might like to add a biography of a Christian woman.

- The men might be willing to purchase a book on being a better husband or father.

Not only do you get a new book for the library that way, but you have a built-in waiting list to read it.

Money Raising Projects

If your church does not object to money raising projects, you have the whole range from yard sales and bake sales to car washes from which to choose. Let your library committee sponsor one of these.

A few months after the library opens, you might hold a "book fair" with your local Christian bookstore. This gives them a chance to show their stock and gives your members a chance to buy for you and themselves. Books make great Christmas and birthday gifts for all ages.

The store should also give you a small percentage of the sales for hosting the fair. Invite the public, and especially let other churches know about it.

The Second Part of Your Mission

Now you also have to get people to use the library more. Without borrowers, the library will die on the vine and stop serving the church, the people and the Lord.

James tells us that "faith without works is dead" (James 2:26). So, too, your library is dead if no one uses it, even if the room, books and historical material are still all there.

When you had your Grand Opening, you invited the Sunday school classes to come in one at a time. Try this again. This time feature the new books.

Ask if anyone wants to mention the book(s) he or she has read from the library, and how they liked it. (To keep a deep silence from descending, you might want to set this up ahead of time with a reader in the class! Just make sure they've actually read the book!) When people of any age see others like them using the library, they will be more inclined to as well.

Take the Library to the People

While you want people to come to the library, you can also take a part of it to them. Put some books on a cart (even a tea cart will do if it doesn't rattle when you push it), and wheel it into some of the meetings in the church and the after services coffee hour. Let people take the books out right then and there.

From taking books to various church locations, it's a small step to taking books to shut-ins and even those in nursing homes. Your committee can do this, but you can also ask for volunteers from the congregation. Those who have relatives or friends they visit often are good prospects for your "traveling library."

For the first visit to someone not able to be in church, choose a variety of books you think they would like. Make a copy of the books in the library, and let the second visit be an individual "as ordered" selection.

By taking the books in person, you can pick up the already read ones and get them back to the library safely. Expect, though, to lose a few from others borrowing them or the reader not knowing where they were put. It's a small price to pay for the joy you bring to the shut-ins.

If the volunteer taking the books to older members is agreeable, have them take a tape recorder or video camera and talk to the older person about your church in the past. You and your committee can come up with some questions to get the person started talking, then let them tell what they remember ... about everything and anything that comes to their minds. The tapes will be a valuable part of your archives.

Fit the Books to the Reader
Be interested in everyone's individual likes and dislikes. It's hard to turn down someone who approaches you with a book, smiles, and says, "I came across this in the library and thought of you right away. I think you'll like it."

Keep Your "Wish List" Up to Date
While you want to buy new books as they come out, there are also older books you need to fill out parts of your library—more study books, references, and other books that don't ever get old.

Put these on your "wish list," and let everyone know what they are. Ask people to watch for them at yard sales, flea markets and used book sales. Keep the same criteria: They must be in good shape.

Chapter Eight

LOOKING TO THE FUTURE

Almost a year has passed since your church library/archives had its Grand Opening. You have learned a lot in these past months.

Volunteers have been found to "man" the room Sunday mornings; money has come in to help with library expenses. A few books have been lost, but not as many as you had expected, and most of these were paid for by the persons who lost them.

People know where the library/archives room is, you plan another "Library Sunday" to celebrate its birthday, and you and your committee are keeping up to date on new books through the Christian bookstore and the publishers' catalogs you have asked to receive. Things seem to be running smoothly. Now it's time to sit back, relax and let the project run itself, right? *Wrong!*

Now is *not* the time to sit back and take your ease as did the rich fool Jesus told about in Luke 12:19. Now is the time to press forward with the same vigor and zeal you started with.

Getting on the Church Budget
If you are not already a part of the church's overall budget, this should be one of your top priorities. If you are already getting some

funds, but think you should have more, now is the time to approach your church's governing board. But don't come unprepared!

Make a Formal Report

- Put all the information about the library/archives on paper. Send this report to the board and to any individuals or organizations that have given you money or other donations this past year.

- Include the amount you have spent on books, supplies and miscellaneous. List the number of books bought or donated, all the memorial books given, and the number of books in each category that were borrowed.

Tell Them What You Need

Jesus told His followers they should count the cost before starting to build (Luke 14:28). You must figure out how much you need to keep the library/archives stable this second year, instead of repeating the financial ups and downs you've had so far.

- A suggested amount for the church library can be figured several ways. Some churches use a percentage (usually 1/2 to 1 percent) of the total budget. Take your church's budget and determine what this would be. If, judging from your expenses this year, the amount seems too high or low, propose a more realistic figure.

- Other churches base the library's budget on the number of people on the rolls (usually more than come Sunday mornings!) or the number in Sunday school classes. If your church is small, perhaps a dollar a year for each person in Sunday school is not enough. Be frugal, but not tight, in your estimate. The chances that the amount you ask will be cut are greater than its being raised.

What Else Do You Want to See in the Library?

As your library grows and is used more frequently, people will begin to ask about things other than books. They'd like to borrow (and donate) videos, CDs, tapes, magazines, and even art and games.

You may also be dreaming of a computer for the library. Your church probably already has a computer set-up, and you may be able to have a terminal at minimum cost. The card catalog (now in the file box) can be put in the computer along with records of expenses and income, and what the money was spent for. In fact, all your records can be kept here.

A computer in the library could also be used for games, Bible study and general information.

Vision for the Future

There are now thousands of churches in this country with working libraries and more that want to start one. You are one of the fortunate ones who have started and kept up a library/archives.

Dare to think *big* about what you want to see for it in the next few years. Remember Paul's advice that he who "soweth sparingly shall reap also sparingly; and he which soweth bountifully shall reap also bountifully" (2 Corinthians 9:6).

And remember Jesus' promise that "if ye shall ask anything in my name, I will do it" (John 14:14).

So don't be afraid to think big, dream big and ask big. The best is yet to come!

Appendix A

CHURCH LIBRARY ASSOCIATIONS

All of the following church library associations can offer help and brochures. They also conduct annual conferences for church librarians.

Church and Synagogue Library Association
P. O. Box 19357
Portland, OR 97280
1-800-LIB-CSLA
http://www.worldaccessnet.com/~CSLA

Evangelical Church Library Association
P. O. Box 353
Glen Ellyn, IL 60138
(630) 681-7591
http://members.aol.com/ECLAssoc/index.html
e-mail: eclalib@aol.com

Lutheran Church Library Association
122 W. Franklin Ave. #604
Minneapolis, MN 55404-2474
(612) 870-3623
FAX (612) 870-0170
e-mail: LCLAHQ@aol.com

Appendix B

DEED OF GIFT SAMPLE FORM

I, _____(Donor's Name)_____, hereby donate to the library/archives of _____(Your Church's Name)_____ the following materials:

(LIST OF DONATED MATERIALS)

I am the owner of these materials and now convey to _____(Your Church's Name)_____ legal title, property rights, and all rights which I have in them.

_____(Your Church's Name)_____ may dispose of any materials determined by its representatives to be of no value to them, provided that prior to any disposal, and during my lifetime, I shall be notified of such appraisal, and that at my request the materials scheduled for disposal shall be returned to me.

Signed _____, Donor

Date _____

This gift is accepted by _____(Your Church's Name)_____, subject to the terms and conditions noted above.

Signed _____, Church Representative

Date _____

NOTES